PEACE and BREAD

The Story of Jane Addams

Stephanie Sammartino McPherson

CAROLRHODA BOOKS, INC./MINNEAPOLIS

To Janis, Joseph, and Jonathan

Library of Congress Cataloging-in-Publication Data

McPherson, Stephanie Sammartino.
  Peace and bread : the story of Jane Addams / Stephanie Sammartino
McPherson.
      p.   cm.
  Includes bibliographical references and index.
  Summary: A biography of the woman who founded Hull-House, one of the
first settlement houses in the United States, and who later became involved in
the international peace movement.
  ISBN 0-87614-792-9
  1. Addams, Jane, 1860-1935 — Juvenile literature. 2. Social workers — United
States — Biography — Juvenile literature. 3. Women social reformers — United
States — Biography — Juvenile literature. [1. Addams, Jane, 1860-1935. 2. Social
workers.] I. Title.
HV40.32.A33M36   1993
361.3′092—dc20
[B]   93-6736
                                                CIP
                                                AC

Manufactured in the United States of America

1 2 3 4 5 6 – P/JR – 98 97 96 95 94 93

CONTENTS

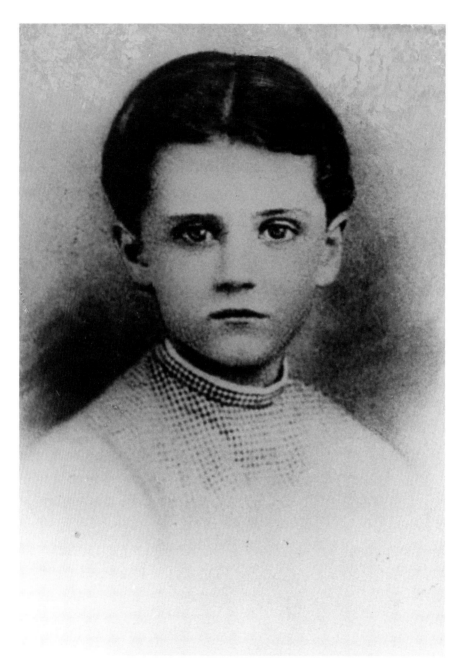

Jane Addams, or Jennie as she was called then, was about six years old when this picture was taken. She was born on September 6, 1860.

I
Growing Awareness

Four-year-old Jennie Addams had discovered a mystery. Why had someone put two American flags on the gate-posts in front of her house? And why had someone decorated the flags with black ribbons? Surely, this had to mean something. Jennie was determined to find out what.

There was one person, Jennie knew, who could tell her about the flags. That was her father, John Huy Addams. To Jennie, he seemed the strongest, bravest, smartest man in the world.

But today John Addams did not try to act brave. To Jennie's surprise and dismay, she found her father crying. She had never known that grown-ups could cry. "The greatest man in the world has died," John Addams explained to the frightened little girl. It was 1865, and he had just learned of the assassination of President Abraham Lincoln in Washington, D.C.

Jennie stood watching her father, wishing she knew how to comfort him. She was too young to know much about President Lincoln or the Civil War, which had just ended.

But for the first time, she began to think about the world beyond the big house where she lived with her father and older sisters and brother. She began to think of the world beyond the small town of Cedarville, Illinois. What happened in the big world must be very important if it could make her father cry.

Because her mother had died when she was only two, Jennie was especially close to her father. A prosperous miller, banker, and state legislator, Mr. Addams was well known in the community. When he moved to Cedarville, it had been little more than a scattering of cottages and open prairie. Jennie's father had helped found the first library, the first church, and the one-room schoolhouse. Mr. Addams was a busy, serious man. But he had a smile and a twinkle in his eye when Jennie climbed on his lap and called him "Pa."

The other Addams children, Mary, Martha, Weber, and Alice, were much older than Jennie. At nineteen, Mary was in charge of the house and her youngest sister. She made sure the little girl had clean clothes and kept out of trouble. But Jennie went to her father, not Mary, when she was worried or confused. His approval meant more to her than anyone else's.

Jennie was so proud of her pa that sometimes she felt she could never measure up to him. Although she was a pretty child with wavy brown hair and large brown eyes, Jennie thought she was ugly. She had a crooked back, which kept her from walking straight, and her toes turned inward. When visitors came to the Sunday school where her father taught, she didn't like to be seen with him.

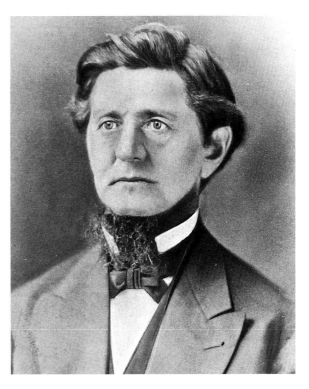

According to Jennie Addams, her father, John Huy Addams, was so honest that bad men feared him.

She couldn't bear for strangers to know that Mr. Addams's daughter wasn't as good-looking and strong as he was.

But Jennie shared her father's intelligence and, more than anything else, his curiosity. About two years after Lincoln died, Mr. Addams took Jennie on a business trip to the nearby town of Freeport, Illinois. There she found herself in a neighborhood unlike any she had ever seen before. The run-down houses around the town's mill were small, ugly, and jammed together like mismatched pieces of a jigsaw puzzle. Jennie was bewildered. Where could the children play in such a cramped, dingy place? Why would anyone choose to live here? And what were these people like?

As usual, Jennie turned to her father for answers. Mr. Addams explained that the people who lived there were poor and couldn't afford to live anywhere else. Jennie didn't want to be poor, but she did wonder what it would be like to live in such a place. "When I grow up," Jennie said, "I will have a large house right in the midst of horrid little houses like these."

Unlike the children in the "horrid little houses," Jennie lived in a large home with fine furniture and a library full of books. From the front windows and second-floor balcony, she could see across a meadow of grazing sheep to the banks of Cedar Creek. There were flowers to pick, birds to watch, and trees to play under. One of the nearby hills was covered with Norway pines from seeds her father had planted when he first came to Illinois in 1844.

Jennie loved her surroundings, but Cedarville was a small, quiet place. Jennie's house was on the very edge of town. Sometimes she couldn't find other children to play with. Sometimes her father was away on business. Jennie was only six years old when Martha Addams died of typhoid fever. Home was suddenly a lonely, sad place. Jennie missed her sister greatly. She worried that Mary would die too. Without Mary, what would she do?

Everyone tried to make Jennie feel safe, and slowly she got over her fears. When Jennie was eight years old, Mr. Addams remarried. Almost overnight Jennie's life began to change. Her stepmother was a tall, handsome woman who liked to dress fashionably, give parties, and entertain important people. Anna Haldeman Addams turned her new home into an elegant showplace, filled

Anna Haldeman (standing on the balcony of the Addams home) married the widowed John Addams in 1868.

with company and laughter. She brought a piano into the parlor and turned dinner into a formal occasion with fancy china and white tablecloths.

At first Jennie didn't know what to make of these changes. She wasn't sure she liked this woman who took up so much of her father's time. When Mary left home for school, Jennie felt very alone.

But Jennie's stepmother was kind as well as strong-minded, and it wasn't long before Jennie was calling her "Ma." Anna Addams encouraged her new daughter to be active in spite of her crooked back. In the evenings, she played the guitar and read plays with Jennie. Best of all, Anna brought two sons into the family. Harry was nearly twenty, but George Haldeman was only six months younger than Jennie.

Jennie and George became fast friends. Now Jennie had someone to share in all her games, someone to walk with down the hill and over the creek to school. When George chased butterflies or caught worms and insects, Jennie went with him. Hunting bugs with George was a real adventure, she discovered. The children roamed the countryside in summer and skated on the millpond in winter. They played chess, killed snakes, and collected black walnuts. Not even Jennie's back could prevent her from climbing up the hillsides with George to explore the caves they found.

Mr. Addams's mills were also good places for adventure. The sawmill was especially exciting, at least when Jennie's parents weren't around. When the coast was clear, Jennie and George liked to hop aboard logs as they moved toward the buzzing mill saw. Heart pounding, head ringing with the noise, Jennie watched the blade spin in front of her. Then, at the last possible moment, she jumped off and watched as the log was sawed in half.

When she wasn't playing with George, Jennie was likely to be curled up in a chair reading a book. John Addams owned many books that Jennie learned to love. She especially enjoyed Charles Dickens's novels and Louisa May Alcott's *Little Women*. She also read history books from her father's library. Mr. Addams paid Jennie twenty-five cents for every volume she read of a famous biography of George Washington and five cents for every biography she read by an ancient Greek writer named Plutarch. This was a good deal of money for those days. But before Jennie could collect, she had to report on what she read.

Students at Cedarville School posed for a class portrait on a warm day in May 1872. Jennie stands second from the left, while her stepbrother George sits in the middle.

Even though Mr. Addams paid Jennie for her book reports, he wanted his daughter to know that there were more important things than money. One cool Sunday, Jennie threw a beautiful new coat over her dress. She was always dressed nicely, but this coat was fancier than anything else she owned. She could hardly wait to show it to her pa and wear it to church.

Mr. Addams agreed the coat was very pretty. Then he added that it was much prettier than the coats of her classmates in Sunday school. Perhaps she should wear her old one, he suggested. It would keep her just as warm and it wouldn't make the other girls wish for things they didn't have.

Jennie was disappointed, almost angry, as she reluctantly took off the beautiful new coat and put on her old one.

Jane in her teens,
with Anna Addams
and George

But walking to church, she remembered her father's words. If everyone had a coat like hers, then she could wear it as much as she wanted. Why did some people have so much more than others? she wondered. Mr. Addams was the richest man in Cedarville, but didn't other children deserve the same things she had? What could be done to even things out?

Mr. Addams wasn't always able to give Jennie a complete answer, but he took her questions seriously. To Jennie, he was a real-life hero. He was so stern, honest, and courageous that bad people were afraid of him and good people looked up to him. Jennie hoped that someday she could make a difference in people's lives just as her pa did. When the end of her days in Cedarville's one-room schoolhouse drew near, she decided to leave the town and see the world beyond.

II
A Wonderful Idea

At seventeen, Jennie was now Miss Jane Addams, a confident and happy young lady. Though she was small, her hope for the future loomed large. Most girls her age were already thinking about marriage and children, but Jane was determined to go to college.

The only question was where. A few colleges in the 1870s admitted both men and women. Some schools just for women had been opened too. But most parents did not feel that their daughters needed to go to college. Young women were supposed to marry and build their lives around their families.

Mr. Addams didn't believe in careers for women, but he did want Jane to go to college. He thought that nearby Rockford Seminary, which her sisters had attended, would be a good school for her.

Jane wasn't so sure. She wanted to go to one of the new women's colleges, Smith College in Massachusetts. Smith offered more classes and was as good as the best men's colleges. Although Rockford was also a good school,

Twenty-one-year-old Jane added a fancy touch to her class picture at Rockford Seminary by grabbing a parasol.

it wasn't a full-fledged college. Instead of degrees, it gave certificates to its graduates. Jane wanted a regular diploma, but she wanted to please her father too. Reluctantly she agreed to go to Rockford.

Jane wasn't disappointed for long. She studied hard, made friends, and learned to love her school. Her room became a popular meeting place. One of her classmates later wrote, "We never speculated as to why we liked to go to her room so that it was always crowded when the sacred 'engaged' sign was not hung out. We just knew there was always something 'doing' where she was."

Jane probably gave copies of this, her graduation portrait, to family and college friends.

Jane was full of ambition and ideas. She helped start a scientific society. She was a member of the debating team, editor of the college magazine, and president of the literary society. Whether she was making a speech or bringing a friend home to visit her family, Jane was exciting to be around. No one was surprised when she was elected president of her class.

The boys at nearby Beloit College liked to be with Jane as much as her classmates did. One young man hoped she would agree to be his wife. George Haldeman, who was also at Beloit, began to think of marrying Jane too.

He tried to show her how his feelings were changing and deepening. But Jane had no thought of settling down as a wife and mother.

Unlike many people, Jane believed women could have happy lives and careers outside the home. "We simply claim the highest privileges of our times, and avail ourselves of its best opportunities," she stated in a speech her junior year. Jane was determined to do something important after leaving college.

In 1881 Jane graduated at the head of her class. She looked forward to a happy summer with her family. Then, in August, a pleasant vacation with her father and stepmother ended tragically. John Addams died suddenly of appendicitis. Jane had lost the most important person in her world.

"The greatest sorrow that can ever come to me has past...," Jane wrote to her college friend Ellen Starr. "I will not write of myself or how purposeless and without ambition I am." But when her first burst of grief was over, Jane realized that her father would not want her to give in to her sorrow.

One month after Mr. Addams's death, Jane enrolled in the Women's Medical College of Pennsylvania in Philadelphia. She had decided while still at Rockford to become a doctor and help the poor. It was a daring decision. For a woman in the 1880s, studying to be a doctor was even more unusual than going to college.

Moving to Philadelphia was a big change for Jane, but she had visited the city as a tourist before. This time, however, Jane had little chance to explore the historic buildings or visit the big stores. She was too busy studying anatomy and medicine.

Jane was a good student and got good grades, but she did not like medical school. She was still grieving for her father, and her curved back began to bother her again. By the middle of the year, Jane's back hurt so much that she had to leave school.

For a time, Jane tried a popular "rest cure" in a Philadelphia hospital. But when she returned home to Cedarville, she still wasn't well. Her back continued to ache, she missed her father, and she was beginning to wonder if she really wanted to be a doctor.

Students work in the laboratory at the Women's Medical College of Pennsylvania in Philadelphia. Jane studied medicine there for a short time in 1881 and 1882.

Jane never returned to medical school or Philadelphia, but she did go back to Rockford for a day. Partly because of her own demands as a student there, the school now gave college degrees. Jane had taken such challenging classes that she had already earned a full diploma. With another girl from the class of 1881, she went through a second graduation ceremony.

Now Jane had the prize she had worked for so hard. But what would she do with it? Before Jane could decide, she had to face her health problem. In the fall of 1882, she agreed to have spinal surgery. Her older stepbrother, Harry Haldeman, was the surgeon. Because Harry had married Jane's sister Alice, he was also her brother-in-law.

For several months after the operation, Jane had to stay in bed at Alice's house in Iowa. Though her sister was a gentle nurse, this was a difficult period for Jane. Not long before, Jane's life had been so full of promise. Now she was worried about her future. Jane read a lot and amused a young nephew by telling him the story of the frog prince over and over. But lying in bed, she could not regain her old confidence.

When Jane was able to return home, Harry designed a special jacket for her to wear under her clothes. It was made of steel and whalebone, and though it supported her back, it also pushed heavily against her lungs. Jane wore the bulky device for over a year. "I guess we can call it a success," she wrote to her sister, "although I do hope it will grow more comfortable in time."

Even when she got used to the jacket, Jane's problems weren't over yet. She had thought about returning to col-

Only a year before this picture was taken, Jane had undergone painful back surgery.

lege, but her brother Weber suffered a mental breakdown. Now Jane was busy sorting out Weber's business affairs and helping his wife. She also had to take care of the investments she had inherited from her father. Jane had property in the Dakota territory, 60 acres of forestland, and a 247-acre farm. But as she took on more responsibilities, Jane's health slowly improved.

In August of 1883, Jane was ready for a new adventure. She and her stepmother were going to Europe. Harry Haldeman thought the trip would be good for Jane's health and nerves. It would also give her a chance to study languages, to see famous works of art, and to discover how people in other countries lived.

Jane was eager to have a good time in Europe. She wanted to see everything—cathedrals, museums, parks, and palaces. But she was also interested in local customs. In London a missionary took some tourists to see the Saturday-night food auction in a poor neighborhood. From her streetcar, Jane watched shabbily clothed men and women huddle anxiously near the produce wagons. These people were desperate to bid their few coins on spoiling vegetables that would not keep until the markets opened again on Monday. Jane watched one starving man sit down in the gutter and immediately begin to gnaw on a dirty cabbage. She was horrified. How could people live this way? she wondered. How did they survive?

Jane continued to visit museums and theaters all over Europe. She wrote long letters home to Weber about the paintings and statues she saw. But still the image of the food auction lodged in her mind.

One winter morning, Jane looked out the window of her little hotel in Saxe-Coburg, Germany. In the town square below, she saw a line of women struggling with heavy wooden containers on their backs. They were carrying a hot liquid used to make beer. Many of the women had scars on their hands and faces where they had been burned by past loads.

Jane couldn't bear to watch them. She hurried down the stairs and darted past the bent women in the square. Storming into the brewery across the street, she sought out the owner. She told him that the women were working too hard and that the containers were far too heavy. There had to be a better way, she insisted.

But the brewer wasn't about to let an excited young American tell him how to run his business. Nothing Jane said about the women and their scars seemed to touch his conscience. Frustrated, Jane returned to her hotel. She couldn't eat the breakfast set before her. All she could think about was the suffering of the women.

Jane and her stepmother spent almost two years in Europe. When they returned to Cedarville, Jane still wasn't sure what to do. Her father had left her enough money to live comfortably even if she never married and never found a job. She could go on helping Weber and caring for her nieces and nephews. But that was not enough for Jane. She had to do something more.

For the next two years, Jane and Mrs. Addams spent summers in Cedarville and winters in Baltimore, where George was a student at Johns Hopkins University. Mrs. Addams enjoyed the social life that the large city offered. She also gently pressured Jane to accept George's proposal of marriage.

This was another difficult time for Jane. She had no romantic feelings for her stepbrother. And she found herself exhausted by the parties, teas, and other events Mrs. Addams expected her to attend. Jane was more interested in exploring Baltimore's charities than in meeting its fashionable people. She had discovered she could spend long hours at orphanages and shelters without feeling tired at all.

Her time with orphans and people in need made Jane do some deep thinking. She knew there were other women like herself with plenty of money and free time but no real sense of purpose. She also knew that many people could not even imagine a life like hers. She thought about people trapped in low-paying jobs and wretched neighborhoods. They could barely afford food and shelter and hardly had a minute to spare.

Jane wondered if there was a way for people like herself to share their daily lives with poor people. Would these two very different groups be able to understand each other? Jane believed they would. She believed that the things people had in common were more important than their differences.

As she sorted out these ideas, Jane continued going to parties, reading, and visiting charities. Finally she and a friend decided to go to Europe, where they would join some other friends, including Jane's college classmate Ellen Starr.

Three days before Christmas in 1887, Jane arrived in England. At twenty-seven, she felt more confident and grown-up than she had during her last trip. As she traveled across Europe, she studied art and languages and went sight-seeing. Then a letter arrived in Rome telling of the death of her sister Mary's daughter, a little girl Jane loved dearly. Jane was heartbroken. Soon afterward she began to suffer severe back pain. For a month, she had to stay in bed while her friends continued their travels. But Jane was determined to recover. As soon as possible, she joined her friends in Spain.

Easter Sunday 1888 found Jane in Madrid, watching one of the nation's most famous sports. Jane had never seen a bullfight before. Fascinated, she watched men on

While traveling in Europe, a confident Jane posed for her portrait.

horseback tease the bull with long wooden spears. Jane's friends were shocked by the cruelty and left early. But Jane didn't flinch when the angry bull killed the riders' horses. She didn't protest when the bull was killed either.

Later, however, Jane was very upset with herself. She thought of the five bulls and many horses that had died. Caught up in the excitement, she had simply sat there, watched the violence, and waited to see what would happen next. With a shock, Jane realized she was doing the same thing in other areas of her life. So much needed to be done in the world, yet here she was still waiting to see what would happen to her next, waiting to discover her life's work.

Jane knew the time had come for action. Even before she traveled to Europe, an idea had been growing in Jane's mind. It was a very vague idea at first, more like a feeling than a plan. She didn't know exactly when it had started. She wasn't sure where it would lead her, but it was a hope for the future.

Jane decided to tell her friend Ellen about her idea. First, Jane explained, she would find a large house in the poorest part of a big city. Then she would invite other young women—like Ellen and herself—to join her. As they helped their neighbors, the women would learn about the real world and its problems firsthand.

This was the first time Jane had shared these thoughts with anyone. Putting her feelings into words seemed an important and risky step. Maybe Ellen would think the idea was foolish. Maybe she would say it wasn't practical at all.

But Ellen understood as well as Jane what it was like to have lots of time and nothing important to do with it. She not only approved of Jane's plan, she wanted to be part of it. Jane was delighted. Suddenly her dream seemed a very real possibility.

Still, Jane had a lot to figure out. She wasn't even sure where to begin. As she toured Spain and northern France, she continued to visit museums, castles, and cathedrals. When she learned that a world conference of missionaries was being held in London, she decided to attend. At Rockford Seminary, Jane had resisted pressure to become a missionary. Now she wanted to talk with people who helped others in foreign countries. They might give her some suggestions for helping people closer to home.

Jane enjoyed the conference, but visiting Toynbee Hall was the best experience of all. Here, fifteen privileged young men, all university graduates, were living and working among the poor. They called themselves settlement workers because they "settled," or made their homes, right in the poor community they wished to serve.

Jane was also fascinated by a neighborhood center in London called the People's Palace. She saw the new swimming pool and gym and toured the meeting rooms and library that had been built in one of the city's poorest areas.

Slowly Jane's ideas began to take a more definite shape. She imagined starting a center like Toynbee Hall in the United States. Perhaps she and Ellen could bring a little beauty into their neighbors' lives. They could share the photographs and art prints they were bringing back from Europe. Ellen, with her teaching experience, might start a few classes.

But Jane knew that would be only a beginning. What would her own role be? Would her new neighbors accept her as a friend? Jane wasn't sure. But she was determined to find out.

III
A Big House
on a Busy Street

Jane pressed her face against the carriage window. A large brick house was just swinging out of view. Solidly built, with a wide porch, it seemed out of place in a neighborhood of dreary shops, saloons, and sad-looking apartment houses. For several months, Jane and Ellen had been searching Chicago for just such a house. But the carriage could not stop. Jane was expected soon in another part of the city.

Chicago in 1889 seemed a perfect place for Jane's plan. It was close to Jane's family and filled with poor people. The city was growing rapidly, as new factories opened and older factories expanded. Sometimes Chicago was called "a city of a million strangers." Most of the people were immigrants and their children. They had left their old homes and countries in search of opportunities and a better life. But when they arrived in the United States, they were often forced to take backbreaking, low-paying jobs and live in crowded, run-down slums.

Jane set out to explore Chicago, to learn more about the people's needs, and to gather support for her plan. Newspaper reporters and charity workers took her to some of the poorest sections of the city. Church groups, missions, and women's clubs listened to her explain her plan to live among the poor. Their suggestions and what she saw for herself helped Jane sharpen the focus of what she wanted to do. She knew she couldn't end poverty, but she could give her neighbors a beautiful place where they might escape, even for a short time, from their drab homes and boring jobs.

First, however, she had to find a place to live. Jane knew that her new home had to be big and well built. It had to have one or two large rooms where many people could gather. Most important of all, it had to be located right in the midst of the people she wanted to help. As her carriage rolled by, Jane wondered if perhaps the search was over. The house she had spied looked large enough and grand enough to be a mansion.

The next day Jane returned to the area to look for the house again. But it was no use. The house seemed to have vanished from Chicago.

Three weeks later, Jane was still seeking any big house in a poor neighborhood. On Halsted Street, she suddenly found herself staring at the same building she had seen from the carriage. Jane could hardly believe her good fortune. This time she made sure she learned all about the house. Built in open countryside by a wealthy businessman named Charles Hull, the house had fallen on hard times when the city grew around it. Now it was

The house on Halsted Street, not long after Jane Addams and Ellen Starr moved in. Note the streetcar tracks in the foreground and the neighborhood children on the front porch.

sandwiched between a funeral home and a saloon. The first floor had been converted to offices and warehouses, and a factory pressed close behind the building. But Jane saw beyond the dirt and disorder. The old house had everything she was looking for.

Jane arranged to rent the second floor and a room on the first floor from Helen Culver, the current owner. Then Jane and Ellen set about restoring and decorating the old rooms. They brought in some good pieces of family furniture and set out their European photographs and prints of famous paintings. Jane displayed the silver that had belonged to her parents. Whatever else this house turned out to be, it was her home, and she was going to make it beautiful.

Even before Jane moved in, news of her plan began to spread. Newspapers and magazines told the story of Jane's plans to help the poor by living among them. The idea of settlement houses like Toynbee Hall was just beginning to take hold in the United States. Not charities or missions, settlements were more like homesteads in the middle of the slums. The educated, middle-class people who lived in settlement houses were surrounded by conditions as new to them as the wilderness must have been to the first pioneers. But these young volunteers were determined to understand and help their neighbors.

On September 18, 1889, just twelve days after her twenty-ninth birthday, Jane moved into 335 Halsted Street with Ellen and their housekeeper, Mary Keyser. Jane was still not certain what she would do or what would happen next. Neither were her neighbors. This part of Chicago, called the Nineteenth Ward, seemed the last place two well-dressed, refined young ladies would choose to live.

"The streets are inexpressibly dirty," Jane told a friend. Trash, rotten fruit, and sometimes even dead animals clogged the pavement. Rats and flies bred in the garbage. Many houses had no indoor plumbing. Street lamps were few, schools were overcrowded, and fire escapes were nonexistent. "One is so overwhelmed by the misery and narrow lives of so large a number of city people, that the wonder is that conscientious people can let it alone," Jane wrote to George Haldeman that fall.

Alone in their house that first night, Jane and her two companions were filled with excitement. A great, new adventure was about to open before them. Soon, they hoped, the empty house would be filled with people.

When she woke up the next morning, Jane discovered that she had left a side door unlocked and wide open. Anyone could have crept in during the night to rob her. But not a thing had been touched. Jane found her photos, silver, and little treasures just as she had left them.

She felt safe in her new home. But some of the neighbors were suspicious of Jane and Ellen. Were they simply do-gooders who didn't know what they were getting into? What could they be thinking?

The streets of Chicago's Nineteenth Ward were "inexpressibly dirty," Jane discovered.

Soon someone decided to find out. Jane and Ellen happily greeted their first guest, a woman whose mother had fallen on hard times in America. They listened to her story and wondered how they could help. Before long other neighbors came to call. Italian, Polish, German, Irish, and Russian immigrants stopped in. Now Jane could get to know the neighborhood. Every day she met people from all over Europe without even leaving the Nineteenth Ward of Chicago.

Many women who came to visit brought their small children with them. Sometimes the children were left to visit by themselves while their mothers hurried to jobs. Jane realized these children needed a place to play and learn. Quickly Jane and Ellen found a young volunteer, Jenny Dow, to organize a kindergarten class in the parlor. In less than a month, twenty-four children attended the kindergarten, and seventy more children were on the waiting list. Soon there were groups for older girls and boys and clubs for young working men and women too. The hallways rang with their footsteps and chatter.

Jane especially wanted to help the children because she remembered the green fields and hillsides of Cedarville. She remembered the wonderful games that lasted day after day, sometimes season after season. Right away Jane realized that the neighborhood children had no place to play. But at Christmas she saw that some children had an even worse problem.

Jane wanted her first holiday in Chicago to be special. She bought books about Abraham Lincoln for a boy's club, shoes for some of her neediest neighbors, and candy

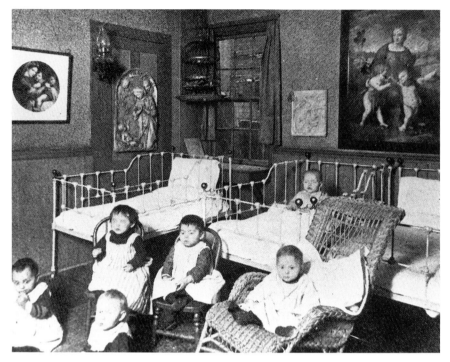

Jane and Ellen soon realized that the children in their neighborhood needed help most of all. A day nursery was one of their first projects.

for the children. She kept her doors open and warmly welcomed visitors. But several little girls were horrified when Jane offered them Christmas candy. Jane herself was even more horrified when they explained why. The children worked fourteen hours each day in a candy factory. When they staggered home exhausted at nine o'clock each night, they were sick of candy. They told Jane they couldn't even bear the sight of it.

Of course, Jane had known in a general way that her neighbors were overworked and underpaid. But she hadn't known about the harshness of child labor. She hadn't known how badly some immigrant families needed the money their children earned. With all her knowledge of art and beauty, she hadn't known much about poverty at all when she came to Halsted Street. Now she was learning that many poor youngsters needed more help than she could possibly give them.

Older people in the neighborhood had problems too. Often they were lonely, sick, and unable to work. Many missed their homes in Europe. On January 1, 1890, Jane held an old settlers' party just for them. It was a time for them to make new friends and enjoy Jane's hospitality. It was also a time for Jane to learn more about her older neighbors and listen to their stories. The party was so much fun that it became an annual event.

From morning to night, there was always something for Jane to do—a neighbor to talk to, a child to tend to, a call for help to answer. "The memory of the first years...is more or less blurred with fatigue," Jane wrote twenty years later, "for we could of course become accustomed only gradually to the unending activity and to the confusion of a house constantly filling and refilling with groups of people."

As the house filled up with neighbors, it also attracted new volunteers. Jane was certain the settlement could be as important to the volunteers as it was to the people in the neighborhood. Often college women wanted to use their education outside the home but didn't know how. Jane felt that she could give them a chance. At her house, volunteers cared for children, taught English, led clubs, and sat down with their neighbors for a chat and a cup of hot coffee or tea.

Jane greets neighbors.

But some immigrants continued to be baffled by the new volunteers. Why would they choose to live and to work in a slum? One puzzled old man told Jane it was the strangest thing he could imagine. But Jane did not feel strange in her new home. She felt happy and energetic and useful. What could be more ordinary and right than helping people? she thought. Gradually Jane's neighbors came to look upon her as someone they could count on. Even the old man finally admitted that the settlement was "not strange, but natural."

IV
A Good Neighbor

At the house on Halsted Street, Jane sometimes felt like a doctor on call. One afternoon she was asked to help a young woman who was having a baby. Neither Jane nor volunteer Julia Lathrop knew much about childbirth, but they rushed to the woman's house. By the time the doctor arrived, they were giving the healthy baby boy his first bath.

Another time an urgent message sent Jane hurrying to a nearby home. An old German woman was about to be taken to the poorhouse. With all her strength, the woman clung to her dresser while her breath came in sharp, irregular gasps. She was terrified at the thought of leaving her home. Jane spoke kindly to the woman and firmly to the officials. She and several other neighbors promised to take care of the woman, and she was allowed to stay.

People who least expected help were sometimes startled by Jane's kindness. One night Jane awoke to find a dark shape moving in the silvery moonlight of her bedroom. Jane knew at once it was a burglar, but she wasn't afraid.

"Don't make a noise," she whispered, worried that the man might waken her young visiting nephew. The burglar was more flustered than Jane. He started to swing himself back over the windowsill, but Jane suggested he use the door instead. It would be much safer than climbing down from a second-story window, she pointed out. The thief tiptoed obediently down the stairs, glad to be off so easy. Several months later, Jane surprised another thief in her house. She promised to find him an honest job if he came back in the morning. Sure enough, the burglar returned the next day, and Jane found him work.

Helping people like the old woman and the burglar was important to Jane. But sometimes Jane couldn't find the space or money for her projects. She had to go beyond the Nineteenth Ward to the wealthy people who believed in her work and were willing to contribute to it.

One important donor was Jane's landlady, Helen Culver. In 1890 Helen donated the entire house and some nearby land rent-free for four years. Now Jane and Ellen could really expand. In appreciation, they named the settlement Hull-House, after Helen's relative.

The first addition to Hull-House was an art gallery, built in 1891 and paid for by a generous donor. Working men and women flocked to see the paintings and to read in the small library on the first floor. With jobs and families to take care of, they had little time to spare. Still, they longed for some beauty in their lives.

Jane understood these longings. She never forgot the wonder and delight of an Italian woman who found a bowl of roses at Hull-House. How amazing, the woman declared, that flowers should come all the way from Italy and look so fresh! When Jane tried to explain that the flowers had been grown in the United States, the woman wouldn't listen to her. For six years, she had lived in Chicago and never seen roses, she said. But when she lived in Italy, she had seen countless roses every summer.

For some immigrants, Hull-House became a home away from home. "Our family lived in four small rooms," recalled an immigrant who grew up near Hull-House. "Half the week, during the winter; the rooms were filled with laundry. Since the clothes were all wrung by hand, it took several days to get the clothes dry. It was no place in which to entertain friends, so while I ate and slept there, I really lived at Hull-House."

The settlement was important to another neighbor, Mary Kenney, for a different reason. On her first visit to Hull-House, Mary was amazed by the spacious hallway, the grand stairway, the high ceilings, and the well-furnished rooms. It didn't seem like the home of someone who would have much in common with a person like Mary, who worked all day in a bookbindery.

But Jane greeted the tall, red-haired girl like an old friend. Then she asked if there was anything she could do to help the bookbinders' group. Mary was surprised that Jane knew and cared about the union she had organized to work for better pay and shorter hours. "We haven't a good meeting place," Mary replied at once. "We are meeting over a saloon on Clark Street and it is a dirty and noisy place, but we can't afford anything better." Immediately Jane offered her Hull-House as a meeting place.

Later Mary Kenney wrote, "When I saw there was someone who cared enough to help us in our way, it was like having a new world opened up."

Soon afterward Jane and Mary were organizing a boardinghouse near Hull-House for working girls. They named it the Jane Club. Club members, or "Janes," as they were called, shared expenses for food, paid low rents, and had many good times together.

Few people in the neighborhood had such comfortable rooms as the Janes. Most landlords cared more about the rent than about their tenants. But one day a landlord came to ask Jane for help. William Kent, a young businessman, had been shocked to learn that he owned several badly run-down apartment houses in the neighborhood. He had inherited the buildings recently and knew very little about them.

Jane sympathized with Mr. Kent, but she also knew the conditions in his apartments were wretched. Together she and Mr. Kent went to see the buildings. They were every bit as miserable as Jane expected. Repairs would be difficult and costly. Dismayed, Mr. Kent offered the buildings to Hull-House.

But Jane didn't want the buildings. She had a better idea. Hull-House would accept the property if Mr. Kent would pay to have the slum apartments torn down. At first he refused. Jane's terms seemed outrageous. But soon he realized she was asking for her neighbors—not for herself.

Even then Jane was not through with Mr. Kent. She convinced him to buy play equipment for the empty lots.

Soon Jane was watching happy children soar on the
swings, climb to the top of the slide, and dig in the sand-
box. Thanks to Jane Addams and William Kent, Chicago
had its first playground.

Chicago's first public playground was built near Hull-House.

Something exciting was always going on at Hull-House
—classes, lectures, and clubs of all sorts. The more Jane
did, the more it seemed there was to do. From her early
morning glance at the mail to dinner with the volunteers
who lived at Hull-House, Jane rarely had time to rest.
Even when she was talking, she couldn't keep still. A
hundred small details claimed her attention. It wasn't
long ago that Jane had been considered an invalid. Now
she somehow found the energy to do everything.

The settlement movement was growing and gaining energy too. By 1900 there were over one hundred settlement houses in the United States. Meanwhile Hull-House was capturing the imagination of people all over Chicago and the entire nation. Schools, church groups, and women's clubs asked Jane to come and speak. She traveled as far as Boston and San Francisco to talk to students, teachers, social workers, and other interested people.

Many people wanted to see Jane's work firsthand. Hundreds of visitors, rich and poor, famous and unknown, came to Chicago to see Hull-House. The residents took turns "toting" them around, as they called leading tours. One visitor described the scene: "Through the Hull-House drawing-rooms there passes a procession of Greek fruit vendors, university professors, mayors, aldermen, club-women, factory inspectors, novelists, reporters, policemen, Italian washerwomen, socialists . . . big businessmen . . . English members of Parliament, German scientists, and all other sorts and conditions of men from the river wards of the city of Chicago and from the far corners of the five continents."

Some of the visitors were curious about Jane Addams. Where was she born? they wanted to know. How old was she? Why didn't she ever get married? What made her decide to start Hull-House?

Sometimes, looking around at the lovely rooms, a visitor asked where the poor were. Then the volunteer doing the "toting" explained that poor people didn't live at the settlement at all. They came there to relax, take classes, and make new friends.

Boys' club members (above) and young actors (right) made Hull-House their second home.

Immigrants gather in a Hull-House classroom to learn about becoming U.S. citizens.

From poor newsboys to famous leaders, Jane treated everyone with the same courtesy and attention. "She never made one feel that she was doling out charity," recalled an immigrant. "When she did something for you, you felt as if she owed it to you or that she was making a loan that you could pay back."

V
The Fight for Social Justice

Occasionally the people who came to Hull-House stayed. One December day in 1891, Jane answered the doorbell and found a Kickapoo man and a middle-aged white woman on her doorstep. Jane was cradling a baby in her arms and was trying to stop a kindergartner from running into the snow, but she had a smile and a warm welcome for her guests. Strangers to each other as well as to Jane, Henry Standing Bear and Florence Kelley were glad of the friendly greeting and the breakfast Jane served them. Florence hoped to volunteer, while Henry was looking for paying work. "We stayed," wrote Florence Kelley years later, "Henry Standing Bear as a helper to the engineer several months; and I as a resident seven happy, active years."

Those seven years were important ones for Jane and for Hull-House too. Jane and Florence became close friends. Florence was interested in social reform and often spoke with Jane about the changes that needed to

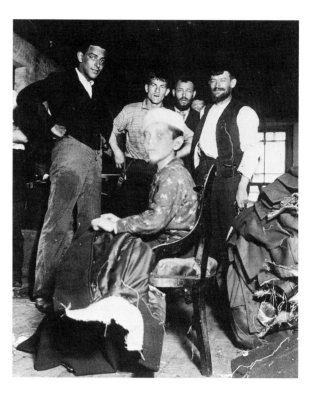

A young boy pulls basting threads in a sweatshop.

be made in society. Soon Jane realized that Hull-House could do more than offer classes and clubs to its neighbors. It could also work for new laws to improve the lives of people all over the state.

Jane Addams, Florence Kelley, and several other residents began to study the way people lived and worked in the Nineteenth Ward. Of course, they already knew what the Hull-House neighborhood was like. Now they set out to prove what they knew to lawmakers and other concerned citizens. They used facts and figures to show how many nationalities lived in the neighborhood, how many people lived in overcrowded slums, and how many children had jobs.

Florence convinced Jane that if they worked hard enough they might be able to end child labor. A new law to stop employers from hiring children under the age of fourteen came before the state legislature in 1893. Florence asked Jane to help get the law passed. For three months, Jane spent every night speaking in favor of the law to clubs, church groups, and trade unions. It was an exhausting schedule, but Jane thought of the children she was trying to help. They were much more tired than she was.

Jane knew that many children worked sixty hours each week in factories and that other youngsters often had to help their mothers with sweatshop jobs at home. In sweatshop work, instead of being paid for their time, workers were paid according to how much they got done. Women spent hours bent over their sewing in dimly lit, stuffy workrooms. Often they brought their sewing home, where their children pitched in to help. "From the age of eighteen months few children able to sit in high chairs at tables were safe from being required to pull basting threads," Florence Kelley recalled.

When the Factory Act passed in 1893, Jane and all the Hull-House residents rejoiced. Now child labor was limited, and women and children could not work more than eight hours per day. Florence Kelley was chosen to become the state's first factory inspector. She opened her office across the street from Hull-House, and many residents helped with her new duties.

Not everyone liked the new law, however. Employers who depended on the large pool of child labor wished people like Jane Addams would stay out of their affairs.

When the Factory Act was repealed in 1895, the Hull-House residents were angry and disappointed. But Jane, Florence, and other volunteers continued to work for new laws and other causes.

Some of the settlement's residents became quite well known. Dr. Alice Hamilton, who came to Hull-House in 1897, studied workers to see how often they became sick from poor job conditions. Julia Lathrop became a member of the Illinois Board of Charities and studied conditions in mental hospitals and county poorhouses. In 1899 she helped establish the first separate court system for children who broke the law. Like the other residents, Julia believed that youngsters arrested for minor offenses should not be treated like hardened criminals. In the juvenile court, helping children to change was more important than punishing them.

Florence Kelley went on to become an officer of the National Consumers' League in New York after leaving Hull-House in 1899. And Ellen Starr, the cofounder of Hull-House, started the Chicago Public School Art Society and opened a bookbindery at the settlement. Although she was best known for her activities in the arts, Ellen had strong political views and was arrested several times for picketing with strikers.

These women and the many other residents were important to Jane as friends as well as coworkers. But her very best friend was a young woman named Mary Rozet Smith. Although Mary did not live at Hull-House, she donated her time and money to the settlement. Her friendship and encouragement meant a great deal to Jane.

Mary Rozet Smith

So did her sense of humor. Jane had been a very serious young woman. But Mary, Florence, and Julia helped her to see the funny side of things.

Jane remained very close to her family. She wrote letters and visited her stepmother and brother and sisters whenever she could. She advised them in their troubles and worried about their problems.

In 1894 Jane's sister Mary became seriously ill. At the same time, strikers threatened to stop train travel across the country. Suddenly Jane was caught between her family and her work. She wanted to be with Mary, but she had also been asked to help end the strike.

The angry strikers worked for the Pullman Company and made sleeping cars for railroads. They did not live in the dirty, crowded streets around Hull-House. George Pullman, their employer, had built them their own town south of the city with comfortable houses and schools, stores, a library, and gyms. It was a pleasant, well-cared-for place, but the workers were required to live there, and rents were high. When Mr. Pullman slashed wages but didn't lower rents, the workers were furious. They voted to go on strike. In a show of support for Pullman workers, the railway union went on strike too. Members refused to run trains that carried Pullman cars.

Open to both sides, Jane Addams tried to understand what had gone wrong. She spoke with Mr. Pullman, had dinner with some of the workers in their model homes, and attended many meetings. But nothing she or anyone else did seemed to help. The strike dragged on.

Fearing Mary would die, Jane left Chicago by carriage to be with her. Sadly, Jane thought of other family members desperately trying to reach Mary from another state. Because so few trains were running, they might not be able to reach her in time. Jane's only comfort was knowing that Mary didn't blame the workers.

After Mary died, a grieving Jane returned to Hull-House, where she found everything in a state of confusion. Troops had been called in to prevent violence from the strike. But their presence had helped spark fighting and destruction. Most of the people who greeted Jane as she walked down Halsted Street wore white ribbons to show support for the strikers. But the Pullman workers were hungry, scared, and upset by the violence. In the end, Mr. Pullman won the strike.

During the Pullman Strike of 1894, members of the Illinois National Guard were called in to keep the peace as tensions mounted.

Jane felt sorry for the strikers and she worried about Mary's children. She wanted to bring her youngest nephew, Stanley, to live with her at Hull-House, but doctors told her it was too dangerous. The danger had nothing to do with violence and strikes. It had to do with garbage.

In the five years Jane had lived at Hull-House, garbage had continued to pile up in the streets. The pavements were littered with dirty rags and overripe fruits and vegetables. Children clambered over the enormous garbage boxes. They hid behind them and reached inside to find pieces of trash to throw at their friends. The smell of the streets made some people feel sick, especially in the hot summer months. Even worse, children ran the risk of infection from playing near the rotting garbage.

Jane had gone to city hall many times to complain. She told nearby families to keep children away from the garbage, wash their hands often, and cover food to protect it from flies. But though conditions improved slightly, flies and germs continued to breed in the heaps of garbage. Rats also made themselves at home.

Jane knew she could protect Stanley by sending him to a clean, safe boarding school. But what about the other neighborhood children who had no place else to go? Jane felt angry and ashamed. Why had she allowed this intolerable situation to go on so long?

Jane began her fight for cleaner streets by taking a good look at the private trash collectors hired by the city. Often these companies cared more about their pay than their job. They let garbage pile up on the sidewalk, and city officials didn't bother to question them. But Jane was about to ask more questions than anyone wanted to answer. With other concerned women, she prowled the streets to check up on the garbage boxes. In just two months, they discovered some very dangerous practices and more than one thousand violations of the health laws.

Armed with these findings, Jane asked to remove the garbage herself, but the city turned her down. Instead the mayor appointed her garbage inspector of her neighborhood. It was the only paying job she ever held. Jane rose at daybreak and climbed into a horse-drawn wagon. In her fresh, white blouse and tidy, long skirt, Jane must have looked out of place as she followed the garbage collectors down the filthy streets. But she was a tough and very determined inspector.

Sometimes trash fell from the wagons. Jane made the collectors pick it up again. She made them add more wagons so that all the trash was collected. She took landlords to court when they didn't supply enough garbage containers for their tenants. And she made sure that dead animals were removed from the streets.

At last Jane made an announcement to the Hull-House Woman's Club. The Nineteenth Ward no longer had the third highest death rate in Chicago. It had dropped to seventh place. The women broke into applause.

Jane would have liked even cleaner streets and an even lower death rate. She knew the main reason for the dismal conditions was the corruption of city politicians. For several years, she tried to get rid of Alderman Johnny Powers by supporting other candidates against him. Mr. Powers, who controlled the Nineteenth Ward, was a greedy and dishonest man. But Jane never succeeded in removing him from power.

Since moving to Hull-House ten years earlier, Jane Addams had filled many roles. She had led political campaigns, given speeches, raised money, tried to end strikes, and directed the growing settlement.

By the early 1900s, Hull-House had an art gallery, a gymnasium, a children's house, a music school, a new building for the Jane Club, a new coffeehouse, a theater, and apartment-style living space for both men and women. The meeting rooms were constantly full of clubs and classes. And the twenty-five residents were constantly greeting people, directing activities, or studying the neighborhood.

Jane and the other residents grew and changed along with Hull-House. "Life in a settlement does several things to you," Alice Hamilton wrote. "Among others, it teaches you that education and culture have little to do with real wisdom, the wisdom that comes from life experience."

The caring friendship of Jane and the other residents taught something to their neighbors too. As an elderly lady, Hilda Satt Polacheck recalled her first visit to Hull-House. A Christmas party was being held, and at first young Hilda was afraid to attend because she was Jewish. In Poland she had been told that bad things could happen to Jewish children on Christmas. Some friends finally convinced her that she would be safe at Hull-House.

Nervously Hilda went to the party. Her eyes grew wide at the sight of the two Christmas trees on either side of the fireplace. But Hilda was even more amazed by the warmth and tolerance she found at the settlement. "As I look back, I know that I became a staunch American at this party," Hilda remembered. "I was with children who had been brought here from all over the world. . . .We were all poor. Some of us were underfed. Some of us had holes in our shoes. But we were not afraid of each other. What greater service can a human being give to her country than to banish fear from the heart of a child? Jane Addams did that for me at that party."

VI
Expanding Horizons

Jane felt troubled walking down Polk Street in the spring of 1900. As she waved to her neighbors, young and old, she was thinking of the widening gap between immigrants and their children. Many youngsters thought their parents were out of touch with American ways. But Jane knew the children were out of touch with something equally important. They were so busy trying to be Americans that they didn't have time to learn about their own ethnic traditions.

In the early 1900s, the United States was thought of as a "melting pot," a place where people of many nationalities came together and lost their differences in their common identity as Americans. Jane believed that many differences were worth preserving. The arts and crafts, the folklore, songs, and dances of their native lands were an important part of the immigrants' heritage. These things could enrich American culture. If only there were a way to forge a link between the newcomers and their Americanized children, to bridge the gap between the old and the new.

Then Jane saw an old Italian woman spinning wool in the sunshine outside her home. Bent over her task, the woman spun her yarn in a simple way—one that peasants in southern Europe had used for hundreds of years. Watching her was a little like looking into the past. The woman's children and grandchildren probably worked in factories. But she herself was a form of living history.

Maybe this woman *did* belong in a museum, Jane thought. Wouldn't it be wonderful to have a museum that showed how crafts had developed in different countries through the years? A museum in which her immigrant neighbors could practice their skills and pass them on to others? Maybe young people would be interested in such a place as well.

Smiling, the old woman held up her spindle for Jane to see. The woman had no idea of the plan she had just inspired. But Jane was so excited that she could hardly wait to get to work. Within a month, she had a room all prepared. Then she went out looking for people to work in the museum. Among the people in her neighborhood, she found women skilled in several different ways of spinning wool and weaving cloth. Jane also found people to demonstrate and teach wood carving, painting, and pottery making. Soon the Hull-House Labor Museum was ready to open its doors.

One evening after the opening, a girl named Angelina came to talk to Jane. She had just seen a group of important and admiring visitors surround her mother, a spinner in the Labor Museum. Angelina was surprised and a little bewildered, but she was also proud.

Demonstrating needlework
at the Labor Museum

An Irish immigrant named Francis Hackett later recalled
what made the Labor Museum and the rest of the settlement so special to him. "Hull-House was American
because it was international," he wrote, "and because it
was perceived that the nationalism of each immigrant was
a treasure, a talent, which gave him a special value for
the United States."

But the country in general did not always share the Hull-
House view—especially in times of crisis. In 1901 President McKinley was shot by an anarchist who believed

the government was too powerful. Suddenly everyone who held radical or unpopular ideas was considered a threat to the nation. Innocent people, many of them immigrants, were arrested in Chicago simply because of their beliefs.

When Abraham Isaac, a newspaper editor and political radical, was arrested, his fellow Russian Jewish immigrants were outraged. They knew that Mr. Isaac's newspaper supported extreme political views, but they also knew he had done nothing wrong. His supporters complained bitterly to Jane Addams. They were especially angry that no one was allowed to see Mr. Isaac.

After calling on the mayor, Jane received permission to visit Mr. Isaac. She and a social worker trudged down a dark stairway to a lonely cell beneath city hall. Sixteen policemen surrounded them as they spoke to the prisoner. Jane found Abraham Isaac nervous, tired, and worried, but otherwise well.

Although she couldn't get him released on bail, at least she could tell his friends and family he was all right. When Mr. Isaac was finally released, many people criticized Jane for helping him. Some even pitched rocks through the Hull-House windows.

In spite of such feelings, the settlement continued to prosper. It was a place where almost any kind of interest could be developed. Hull-House offered English, citizenship, and college-level classes. There were also reading clubs, dancing classes, gym classes, and lectures. The Hull-House Theater put on shows, and the music students gave concerts.

Evening Clubs and Classes...January 15, 1895.

MONDAY EVENING.

8.00	Lincoln Club	Miss Barnum	Lecture Hall.
7.00	Art History	Miss Starr	Dining Room.
8.00	Odyssey	Miss Starr	Dining Room.
7.00	German	Mr. McFadden	Library.
8.00	German	Mr. McFadden	Library.
7.30	Drawing	Miss Benedict	Studio.
7.00	Gymnastics (Men)	Mr. Pierson	Gymnasium.
8.00	Granite Club	Mr. Vanderlipp	Art Exhibit Room.
		Mr. Harding	
7.30	School Girls' Club	Miss Pratt	Miss Trowbridge's R'm.

TUESDAY EVENING.

8.00	Social Science Club	Dr. Brooks	Lecture Hall.
8.00	Henry Learned Club	Miss West	Dining Room.
7.00	Emerson Class	Mr. Arnold	Library.
8.00	Italo-American Club	Mr. Valerio	Art Exhibit Room.
7.30	English and Letter Writing	Miss Crain	Studio.
8.30	English and Letter Writing	Miss Crain	Studio.
7.00	Gymnastics (Women)	Miss Gyles	Gymnasium.
8.00	Mandolin Club	Members	Cottage.
7.30	Cash Girls' Club	Miss Fryar	Miss Trowbridge's R'm.

WEDNESDAY EVENING.

8.00	Anfreda Club	Miss Warner	Lecture Hall.
7.00	Dante	Miss Starr	Dining Room.
8.00	Shakespeare	Miss Crain	Dining Room.
8.00	Lexington Club	Mr. Will	Art Exhibit Room.
8.00	Young Citizens	Mr. Rosenthal	Studio.
7.00	Beginning Latin	Miss Zimmerman	Octagon.
8.00	Advanced Latin	Miss Young	Octagon.
7.30	Gymnastics (Men)	Mr. Pierson	Gymnasium.
8.00	Geometry	Miss Oakley	Laboratory.
8.00	Jolly Boys' Club	Miss Fryar	Miss Trowbridge's R'm.

THURSDAY EVENING.

8.00	Club Lectures		Lecture Hall.
7.00	Singing	Miss Smith	Dining Room.
8.00	Singing	Miss Smith	Dining Room.
7.00	German Needlework	Frl. Hannig	Library.
7.30	Parliamentary Law	Mrs. Lee	Art Exhibit Room.
8.00	Italian Class	Mr. Valerio	Studio.
8.00	Physics	Mrs. Blount	Laboratory.
7.30	Hull-House Glee Club	Miss Anderson	Miss Trowbridge's R'm.
8.00	Laurel Club	Miss Warner	Cottage.
8.00	Gen'l Entertainments	1 Y. P. Clubs	Gymnasium.
		2 Jane Club	
		3 Col. Ex.	
		4 Men's Club	

FRIDAY EVENING.

8.00	General Meetings	1 Civic Federation	Lecture Hall.
		2 M. C. Literary Sec.	
		3 Goodrich Alumnae Association	
		4 M. C. Literary Sec.	
8.00	German Reception	Mr. & Mrs. Goldmark	Dining Room.
8.00	English History	Miss Barton	Library.
7.30	Algebra	Mr. Monroe	Studio.
7.00	Beginning French	Miss Colvin	Art Exhibit Room.
8.00	Advanced French	Miss Colvin	Art Exhibit Room.
8.00	Choral Society	Mr. Tomlins	Gymnasium.
8.00	Mandolin Club	Members	Cottage.

SATURDAY EVENING

8.00	Dancing Class		Lecture Hall.
8.00	Italian Reception	Mr. Valerio	Dining Room.
8.00	Cloak Makers' Union (Women)		Art Exhibit Room.
7.00	Arithmetic	Mr. Chas. W. Mann	Studio.
8.00	Chemistry	Miss Hunt	Laboratory.
8.00	Dancing Class	Miss Browne	Gymnasium.

EVERY MORNING.

	Kindergarten	Miss Paine	Butler Gallery.
		Miss West	
		Miss Buckingham	
		Miss Eaton	

Classes and clubs at Hull-House

With so much going on, Hull-House needed more space. An apartment building with a men's club was built in 1902. Two years later, the Woman's Club Building was completed. A residents' dining hall and the Boys' Club Building followed in the next few years. Land donated by Helen Culver made much of the expansion possible. Old buildings were remodeled or even moved to meet the changing needs. "We used to think nothing," Jane once said, "of moving a building twenty-seven feet west, nine feet south, and fourteen feet up." By 1907, when the new nursery was finished, Hull-House was made up of thirteen interconnected buildings and covered a full city block.

To make room for new volunteers, classes, an art gallery, library, and labor museum, Hull-House grew to cover an entire city block.

As Hull-House grew, so did Jane's horizons. She wanted to see important changes made not just in Chicago or Illinois, but for people all over the country. In a way, weren't they her neighbors too?

Jane realized she could spread her ideas through writing. She began to revise the many speeches she had given during her first ten years at Hull-House. Jane was a careful, precise writer. After a book was typed by a secretary, she got out her scissors and set to work all over again. She cut up the pages, rearranged her ideas and examples, and stuck the papers together again with sewing pins. Over and over again, she reviewed each book until it was as logical and convincing as she wished it to be.

Jane's early books sold well and were praised in newspaper reviews. But it was her autobiography that really captured the public imagination.

In *Twenty Years at Hull-House,* Jane told the story of her childhood, her college years, and the confusion and unhappiness she felt after her father's death. She described her growing awareness of poverty and her decision to found a settlement house.

But Jane wrote about other people besides herself. She wrote about her neighbors—the children who refused candy the first Christmas at Hull-House, the mothers who left their children with her while they went to their jobs, the old people who were lonely and afraid of the poorhouse. Their stories were really Jane's story too. She had given herself to Hull-House, and its success was more important to her than the details of her personal life.

Jane was fifty years old when *Twenty Years at Hull-House* was published in 1910. She had come a long way from the frustrated young woman who hadn't known what to do with her college degree. Now she was a mature and confident woman. Friendly and kind, she was also strong, efficient, and a very good businesswoman. Her gaze was mild and direct at the same time. To some people she seemed remote, even when she was trying to help others. But perhaps that was because she had so many things on her mind. Jane listened to dozens of stories each day and knew thousands of people. Once an old man remarked, "Nobody round here knows me anymore 'cept, of course, Miss Addams." The man had taken Jane's interest for granted, like a basic fact of life.

Jane wrote her best-selling autobiography, *Twenty Years at Hull-House,* in 1910, at about the time this photograph was taken.

By 1910 Jane Addams had become one of the most famous and best-loved women in the United States. She had been named the first woman president of the National Conference of Charities and Corrections and was the first woman to receive an honorary degree from Yale University. She was honored by Smith College, the same school she had once longed to attend. Her popularity was so high that some women's rights supporters even urged her to run for the United States Senate. At a time when women in most states could not even vote, this was an amazing suggestion.

Jane had enough to do at Hull-House without thinking of becoming a senator. But she did find time to work for women's rights. In 1906 Jane had attended her first meeting of the National American Woman Suffrage Association, a group fighting for the vote, or suffrage, as it was called. Jane had met the famous suffragist Susan B. Anthony and had given a speech explaining why women should vote. Living in Chicago's Nineteenth Ward had convinced Jane that women needed the vote in order to protect their communities and children.

Jane became vice president of the same suffrage group in 1911. The next year she spoke again at its convention in Philadelphia. Afterward she led a group of women to Washington, D.C., to try to convince Congress to give them the vote. Jane began her presentation to Congress by talking about what it meant to be a wife and mother. Running a city or a country was a little like running a house and caring for children—only on a much larger scale, Jane believed.

Women demanding suffrage, or the right to vote, often took to the streets in the early 1900s.

When former president Theodore Roosevelt ran for president again in 1912, he supported many social and factory reforms that Jane and other Hull-House residents supported. He also promised to help women get the right to vote.

But Jane was not totally happy with Roosevelt. She was deeply troubled when he refused to let black people take part in his party's convention. Few black people lived around Hull-House, but Jane cared very much about the rights of African Americans. Since 1909 she had been a member of the newly formed National Association for the Advancement of Colored People. "It seems to us inconsistent," Jane declared, "when on one page of our newspapers we find that this party is to stand for the working man and the working woman, and to protect the rights of children. . . and on the next we find that it denies the right of the Negro to take part in this movement."

Despite her anger at such unfairness, Jane decided to support the new party. She believed it would work for many important changes in society, changes that would help both black and white Americans. All over the country, people had the same needs as her Hull-House neighbors. Jane not only accepted the new party, she also gave a speech supporting Roosevelt at the convention.

The large auditorium grew quiet as Jane began to talk. "A great party has pledged itself to the protection of children, to the care of the aged, the relief of overworked girls, the safeguarding of burdened men," she declared. Hundreds of people focused their gaze on the gentle, self-assured woman. They knew these were the same goals she had been working toward for over twenty years.

When she finished her speech and left the platform, several women unfurled a large yellow banner reading VOTES FOR WOMEN and started marching behind her. Other women joined them. Soon Jane found herself at the head of an informal parade. The audience clapped and cheered as Jane Addams passed through the hall. "She is . . . probably the most widely beloved of her sex in all the world," reported one newspaper.

Jane Addams and presidential candidate Theodore Roosevelt shake hands in this cartoon from *The Boston Journal.*

Jane's speech at the convention was only the beginning. Taking to the campaign trail, she spoke in support of candidate Roosevelt from Minnesota to Colorado. Jane had begun the campaign with very little hope that Roosevelt would be elected. By Election Day, she was feeling more hopeful. The crowds had been so enthusiastic. Maybe enough men had listened to her message to make a real difference in the election.

That November, Woodrow Wilson was elected after all, but Jane did not lose heart. The issues had always been much more important to her than the candidate. She hoped and believed that the new president would work for change.

VII
Leader in the Peace Movement

Within two years of Roosevelt's defeat, Jane was involved in a very different kind of campaign—the campaign for peace. In August 1914, war broke out in Europe. Jane and Mary Rozet Smith were vacationing near Bar Harbor, Maine, when they heard the news. In the quiet seaside setting of their summer home, the war seemed far away, almost impossible to imagine.

As the days passed and the grim news reports continued, however, World War I became all too real to Jane. She thought about the thousands of young men fighting and dying in Europe—men who were really no different from her neighbors around Hull-House. She thought of the wastefulness and tragedy of war. The United States had not entered the conflict, and Jane was determined to do everything she could to promote peace.

Many of her fellow women's rights supporters and settlement workers also wanted to end the war. That September, Jane attended a meeting for pacifists, or people opposed to war, at the Henry Street Settlement in New York City. She told reporters that even her efforts to end child labor seemed insignificant compared to her efforts to stop the war.

Just as she believed women could play a special role in social reform, Jane also felt women should work together for world peace. With women's rights leader Carrie Chapman Catt, she wrote a letter to national women's groups inviting members to a conference in the nation's capital. On January 15, 1915, three thousand women met in the ballroom of a hotel in Washington, D.C. Jane gave the opening speech, led all the sessions, and became the leader of the new Woman's Peace party. "We demand that women be given a share in deciding between war and peace," the new group said in a statement.

The next month a group of women in Europe asked Jane to chair an international peace congress of women. At the congress in The Hague, Netherlands, women from countries at war and countries at peace would have a chance to meet and work together. Perhaps they could create a framework for peace in Europe.

But such a conference could also create problems, Jane thought. An international gathering might seem disloyal to people who put their own country's interests above peace. "The undertaking, of course, offers many possibilities of failure," Jane wrote to Lillian Wald, the head of the Henry Street Settlement. "Indeed, it may even do much harm." But if Jane had serious doubts about what the congress could accomplish, she had no doubts that she would attend. She was willing to take a gamble for peace.

Jane (front row, second from left) doubted that peace delegations to Europe would do any good in ending the First World War, but she was always willing to try.

Forty-two other women, among them Hull-House resident Alice Hamilton, joined Jane as she set forth for the Netherlands. It was a dangerous time to be crossing the Atlantic. German submarines patrolled the ocean. Even the weather seemed against the women, as the ship tumbled through rough, rolling seas. At first Jane's mood was as dismal as the weather. She was seasick and worried. But soon a sense of adventure and companionship replaced Jane's gloom. The other women were as dedicated and determined as she was. Jane and her companions spent most of their time discussing the causes of the war and the issues to be covered at The Hague.

Whatever doubts Jane originally had about the congress vanished as soon as she arrived in The Hague and the meetings got under way. One thousand official delegates from twelve nations attended, but often the number of women soared to over two thousand. The largest hall in The Hague was needed to hold them all.

"The great achievement of this congress," Jane explained to a reporter, "is the getting together of these women from all parts of Europe when their men folks are shooting each other from opposite trenches." At The Hague, everyone was on the same side—the side of peace.

Jane was a capable and inspiring leader. The women at the congress believed that the nations not at war could play a key role in bringing peace to Europe. They wanted neutral countries to work with the warring nations and suggest peace terms acceptable to everyone.

The congress decided to send two small groups of women to discuss its goals with world leaders. Jane had not favored this plan. To her, it seemed an almost hopeless errand. What good could possibly come from face-to-face visits? she wondered when she was chosen to visit the warring nations. But so many people thought it was a good idea that she agreed to go. "I don't think I have lost my head," she wrote to Mary Rozet Smith. "There is just one chance in 10 thousand. . . . You can never understand unless you were here, how you would be willing to do anything."

Two days before Jane Addams began her peace mission, German submarines sank the British ship *Lusitania*. Nearly 1,200 people died, including over 100 Americans.

Now more Americans were clamoring to enter the war. Jane was as outraged as anyone, but she was still committed to working for peace. Outwardly calm, but inwardly nervous, she met with British prime minister Asquith and Sir Edward Grey in London. The men greeted Jane Addams courteously, but they offered no false hopes. They believed that only a military victory could end the war. Jane wondered aloud if her visit appeared absurd to them. "Not at all," came the prompt reply. "It may be of some good. At any rate it is worth trying."

In Amsterdam, Jane and Aletta Jacobs, the Dutch physician and suffragist who had organized the congress, met Alice Hamilton and Frau van Wulfften Palthe from Germany. Together the four women traveled to Berlin, Vienna, Budapest, Rome, Berne, and Paris. With the exception of the French officials, Jane found the government leaders ready to listen. "Each one said that his country would be ready to stop the war immediately if some honorable method of securing peace were provided," Jane later recalled.

Prime Minister Sturgkh of Austria went so far as to call the plan "the first sensible words that have been uttered in this room in ten months." And in Rome, Pope Benedict XV, leader of the Catholic church, spent forty minutes telling the women of his sadness at the war and asking them about their plan.

But all this was not enough. Jane returned home without anything definite to show for her efforts. A great deal, she knew, would depend on President Wilson. She hoped he would call a peace conference.

Jane went to the first International Congress of Women at The Hague with many doubts about its usefulness. But at this and later meetings she became committed to the cause of peace.

Jane was greeted enthusiastically when her small steamer landed in New York City. Several days later she spoke to more than 3,000 people at Carnegie Hall about her experiences in Europe. Jane wanted to show that most soldiers didn't want to kill their fellow men, that they were horrified by the reality of war. In her speech, she said that before battle soldiers often drank liquor to help them fight.

But Jane's attempt to show the decency of the young soldiers was misunderstood. Newspapers all over the country attacked her for saying the soldiers were drunk. They thought Jane was casting doubts on the soldiers' bravery. She was called "foolish" and "a silly, vain, impertinent old maid." One paper declared that Jane Addams was "fast losing the esteem, which her earlier efforts seemed to merit." Confused and saddened, Jane continued to speak out for peace. Public approval was important to her, and she was hurt by the bitter criticism.

Some of Jane's friends feared that all the talk might affect her meeting with President Wilson. Time after time, the interview was put off. But at last Jane got her chance to give the women's peace plan to the president. She told him about her visits to the warring capitals and her belief that the neutral nations could help bring about peace. Although the president listened carefully, Jane couldn't convince him to call a conference to try to end the war.

That summer and fall, Jane continued her peace activities, but she wasn't well. She was fifty-five years old, exhausted, anxious, and suffering from a serious bladder and kidney infection. Jane kept up her hectic pace as long as she could.

In December 1915, Jane was hospitalized with pneumonia and more kidney problems. Barely recovered, she returned to Washington the very next month to testify before Congress. Many members of Congress wanted to start increasing the army and navy in case the United States entered the war. Jane Addams argued against such a buildup.

By now Jane was used to criticism. She was probably not surprised when the press attacked her. Most certainly, she was not ready to give up. Still weakened by her recent illness, she went to see President Wilson again. Jane felt heartened when he pulled out the well-worn sheets of paper she had given him at their last meeting. "You see I have studied these resolutions," the president said. "I consider them by far the best formulation which up to the moment has been put out by anybody." Although Wilson still did not call a peace conference, Jane believed he would keep the United States out of the war.

Many people shared her views, and peace became an issue in the next presidential campaign. In 1912 Jane had persuaded many men to vote for Theodore Roosevelt. Now in 1916, she had the one vote that mattered to her most of all—her own. Although most American women couldn't vote until the passage of the Nineteenth Amendment in 1920, a few states were ahead of the rest of the nation. In 1913 Illinois had passed a law giving women in that state the right to vote.

"The disposition of Miss Addams' first presidential vote is a matter of intense interest to every righteous American," announced one newspaper after she said she would vote for Wilson. The president himself wrote her that "no support could hearten me more than yours." After his election he invited her to have dinner at the White House.

But Jane Addams did not have the president's support when she most desperately wanted it. The next February the United States broke off relations with Germany. The country was one step closer to war. Jane went one more time to see President Wilson, but it was no use. In April 1917, the United States entered World War I.

After Congress declared war, the government put all its energy and resources into winning. Everyone was pressured to support the soldiers and the war effort. A new wave of patriotism swept through the country. Suddenly many pacifists began to change their views. It was one thing to condemn the war when only other countries were involved. It seemed disloyal to oppose it when one's own country was fighting.

Living at Hull-House had taught Jane to see the world in a more international light. Her neighbors came from many different countries. They had different languages, customs, and religions, but they understood and respected each other. Jane knew that understanding was harder to achieve between countries than between neighbors. But she believed it was possible if enough people were dedicated to peace. War, Jane insisted, didn't solve the problems between nations.

Sometimes, however, it seemed as if no one agreed with her. Jane was criticized by the press and felt miserable and alone. Even at Hull-House, she couldn't escape from the war. Most of the residents favored going to war. But at least at the settlement there was respect and tolerance for different opinions.

Many young men who lived near the settlement went off to fight in Europe. Before they left, Hull-House gave them a hearty send-off meal. Reluctantly Jane agreed to have a draft board at Hull-House. The night before the first men signed up to be drafted into the military, she couldn't sleep. She had never imagined that Hull-House would be used this way.

The next morning, Jane watched her young male neighbors line up in the large room that had once been a polling place for elections. With a heavy heart, she wished them a good morning. She wondered how many would be called on to fight. What would their families do without them? Would some of the men die in the trenches?

A bitter Italian man broke into Jane's thoughts. "I really have you to thank if I am sent over to Europe to fight," he said. "I went into the citizenship class in the first place because you asked me to. If I hadn't my papers now I would be exempted." Jane remembered the speech she had given to the man's citizenship class and how cheerfully she had congratulated the new Americans. Now there was little she could say to comfort the man.

Eventually Jane found a way to help people without supporting the war. She joined Herbert Hoover's Department of Food Administration, which worked closely with other countries to share supplies. Jane toured the United States urging women to conserve food. She spoke over and over again about the world food situation. If Americans produced more and wasted less at home, there would be food to share with hungry people overseas, she explained. This was the only way that people in many parts of the world could survive. After the war, Jane discovered the tragic truth of her statements for herself.

VIII
Another Foot of Progress

Driving through the French countryside, Jane saw devastation everywhere. It was April 1919. The war was over, and Jane and her companions—Alice Hamilton, Congresswoman Jeanette Rankin, and settlement leader Lillian Wald—were touring battlefields on their way to Zurich, Switzerland. They were going to attend the second International Congress of Women.

At Vimy Ridge, where many men had been killed, the women's car broke down. Jane and Alice got out and took a sobering walk across the hillside. A cold rain began to fall. They were forced to take cover in a crumbling building overlooking rows of wooden crosses, rusty loops of barbed wire, and three army tanks. It was a desolate sight. As they looked over the hillside, the women felt sure that they had done the right thing in opposing the war.

Several days later, Jane found the grave of her nephew, John Linn. "Here the battlefields were hardly cleared at all," Alice Hamilton later recalled. "One saw tin hats, canteens, knitted socks, lying in the mud as they had fallen. It was mud everywhere, deep, slimy mud, and it rained again and the cold seemed more piercing than ever."

Shivering with grief and cold, Jane said good-bye to her sister Mary's son. She thought of the fine man who had come to Europe as a chaplain, of his twice weekly letters, which ended abruptly only three weeks before the war's end.

After their experiences in France, Jane and her friends were glad to arrive in Switzerland. One hundred and fifty delegates from sixteen countries met in Zurich to talk about peace. But so many other people came to listen that the meetings had to be moved to the biggest building in the city. Jane was deeply upset by the stories she heard of starving children in Germany, central Europe, and Russia. The first thing the congress did was to telegraph Paris, where leaders were working out a peace treaty. The women urged the winning nations to allow food to be shipped to the defeated nations.

An almost electric tension filled the room when Jane Addams, the leader of the conference, announced that a telegram had just arrived from President Wilson. But although the president said he understood their feelings, he did nothing to end the food blockade.

Before the congress ended, the delegates voted to become a permanent organization, the Women's International

League for Peace and Freedom, and Jane Addams was elected president. Soon after the final session, she went to Paris to give President Wilson a list of resolutions passed by the congress.

Jane Addams wasn't allowed to see the president, but she did meet with Herbert Hoover, who was also in Paris. Hoover urged Jane to visit Germany to report on the plight of the starving children and to distribute food. "Germany needs not only food," he said, "she needs people of good will to bring her back to normal relations with the rest of the world."

Jane and her friends entered Germany less than a week after the official peace declaration. Nothing they had seen in France or Switzerland prepared the women for what they found. Wherever they went—to schools, hospitals, camps, and kindergartens—they saw hungry, malnourished children. Years later Alice Hamilton remembered the children's "little sticklike legs, the swollen bellies, the ribs one could count, the shoulder blades sticking out like wings."

Jane looked at the children and felt their hopelessness. The supplies she had brought with her—$30,000 worth of condensed milk, sugar, and other basic foods—were not nearly enough. When she returned to the United States, Jane made speeches asking people to give money for the hungry German children. She told of mothers desperate to buy milk and bread for their families. She described the watery soup almost empty of calories and the bread made of dried bark and sawdust that many youngsters were forced to eat.

But some Americans refused to see beyond the recent war. Nothing could soften the anger they still felt for Germany. They were afraid of anyone who seemed a threat to America. This included Germans and anyone who called for major change in American government or society. Communists, socialists, pacifists, and even some members of women's rights groups were all lumped together in this category.

When foreigners with unpopular political views were arrested and returned to their home countries, Jane was indignant. She respected their right to voice their opinions. "Let us give these people a chance to explain their beliefs and desires," she urged.

Many people not only refused to listen to the radicals, they also refused to listen to Jane Addams. They thought she was a traitor for wanting to help Germany and for defending other "traitors." Again, the newspapers attacked her. Some even called her "the most dangerous woman in America." But she kept on with her appeals for help and for justice.

Throughout the 1920s, Jane traveled and continued to work for the Women's International League for Peace and Freedom. She still directed Hull-House, but she spent more and more time overseas. In 1922 she took a trip around the world with Mary Rozet Smith. Outside the United States, she was as respected and popular as ever. In Japan throngs of people gathered to greet her wherever she went. She was moved and a little embarrassed when five thousand Japanese schoolchildren waved flags in her honor.

Jane (right) and another Chicago settlement worker join a peace demonstration.

Before she left Japan, Jane had surgery to remove a tumor. Although her health was poor, she continued her travels. In 1926 Jane had a heart attack, but two years later she was on her way to Honolulu to head a meeting of the Pan-Pacific Women's Union. In 1929 she went to Prague, Czechoslovakia, for another conference of the Women's International League. Jane loved these gatherings, but they were getting to be too much for her. After the conference, she resigned her presidency. The league gave her the title Honorary President, a position she held for the rest of her life.

The year 1929 also marked the fortieth anniversary of Hull-House. As busy a writer as ever, Jane was working on a new book about her second two decades at the settlement. Called *The Second Twenty Years at Hull-House,* the book covered her work for peace and for women's rights. She also described the changes she had seen in the old neighborhood.

Perhaps the worst change of all was happening even as Jane wrote. America had entered hard times. During the Great Depression, from 1929 to about 1939, jobs were scarce, wages were low, and people were frightened for the future. "I have watched fear grip the people in our neighborhood around Hull-House," Jane said a few years later. "Men and women who have seen their small margin of savings disappear; heads of families who see and anticipate hunger for their children before it occurs." For all Jane's hard work, her neighbors, who now included many Mexicans and blacks, faced worse hardships than immigrants had faced forty years earlier.

Hull-House had to tighten its budget, but Jane refused to be discouraged. "It really is a wonderful time in which to live, in spite of much suffering," she said. By "wonderful" Jane meant the chance to help people, to work for a brighter future, and to push for social justice.

Even as Jane thought of the troubles around her, she wanted to celebrate. Hull-House had been open forty years. This was an important milestone, after all. Jane wanted to share her memories with past residents, old friends, and current neighbors. She wanted to recall the good times, the struggles, the many accomplishments.

Money was tight during the Great Depression, but Hull-House still managed to serve hot food to children in the nursery school, offer art classes, and provide many other services.

Jane and a young
friend at Hull-House
in the early 1930s

Jane's party was one year late, but it was worth the wait. For three days, former residents and neighbors enjoyed the hospitality of Hull-House. There were speeches and dinners. The Hull-House Theater put on plays, the Music School gave a concert, and the Labor Museum set up exhibits. A moving picture team came to record the event in one of the new "talkie" films.

It seemed as if every hallway and corner of Hull-House was filled with people, from the coffeehouse to the court-yard. "Jane Addams moved among the great and humble just as any mother would when her far-flung children returned to the old home for a reunion," recalled a woman who had grown up in the neighborhood. "She knew everybody's name. . . . I felt that all the people who had come to that reunion were her family."

Jane never forgot her "family," but she no longer stayed at Hull-House for the winter. Her health couldn't stand the strain of the harsh Illinois weather. She began spending the coldest months in Arizona, where the climate was warmer and she could relax.

By the 1930s, most newspapers had stopped criticizing Jane for her views. People were beginning to lose their wartime fears and hatreds. They were beginning to appreciate Jane's work again. During the final years of Jane's life, she was praised and honored once more. It was as if the country had forgotten about her opposition to the war. But Jane never forgot her convictions—not even for a minute.

In 1931 Jane Addams received her greatest honor of all—the Nobel Peace Prize. After so much criticism, she was finally recognized for her work to end war around the world. Seventy-one-year-old Jane was hospitalized in Baltimore and couldn't go to Norway to accept the award in person. But her room became an exciting place as piles of telegrams poured in. Jane read each message with quiet happiness. Congressmen, senators, and Herbert Hoover, now president of the United States, sent congratulations.

Jane was the first American woman to receive a Nobel Prize. She donated her prize money, more than $16,000, to the two most important concerns of her life, the Women's International League for Peace and Freedom and her neighbors around Hull-House.

Jane never stopped wanting to make her neighborhood and her world better, but her health was rapidly failing. In May 1935, doctors discovered that Jane had advanced cancer. Several days later she died. Thousands of people jammed into the Hull-House courtyard to pay last respects.

Jane Addams was buried in her hometown of Cedarville beneath the hillside of Norway pines her father had planted ninety years earlier. "Jane Addams of Hull-House and the Women's International League for Peace and Freedom" reads the inscription over her grave.

People jammed into the courtyard of Hull-House to pay their last respects to Jane Addams after her death on May 21, 1935, at the age of 74. The shops on Halsted Street were covered in purple and black crepe. "Purple for the nobility of her life; black for our great loss," a shopowner explained.

In spite of the problems she faced and the tragedies she witnessed, Jane had always remained a hopeful person at heart. "Human beings are becoming more humane," she had said on her seventieth birthday. "But there are always new causes to work for, new conflicts to be resolved and settled, another foot of progress to be made." Jane never ceased to reach for that next foot.

AFTERWORD

Although Jane Addams spent her life helping others, poverty and injustice still exist. The Hull-House residents tried to change these conditions. "But what does [their work] amount to?" a New York newspaper asked in 1912. "A speck in the ocean of misery, suffering, and poverty."

Walter Lippmann, a settlement worker from Boston, agreed. "Hull-House cannot remake Chicago," he wrote. "A few hundred lives can be changed, and for the rest it is a guide to the imagination."

Through the years, some people questioned the settlement's significance even for those "few hundred lives." What difference did reading parties, art classes, and a Labor Museum make when people were still trapped in low-paying jobs and wretched houses?

Jane always thought that such events did make a difference. And she was flexible enough to learn from her neighbors and to change to meet their needs. She fought hard for her neighbors' rights. She also gave them friendship, hope, and a break in their daily routines. There was always something to look forward to at Hull-House, always someone who cared and was ready to listen. If Jane couldn't solve all the problems of her neighborhood or the world, at least she pointed them out. It was an important beginning.

Jane Addams, Ellen Starr, and another settlement worker take tea sometime around 1900 in the Hull-House bookbindery.

Hull-House still stands on Halsted Street, but the old neighborhood is gone. The original house has become part of the campus of the University of Illinois at Chicago. A museum now, it is restored to the way it looked when Jane Addams lived there. Crowds of students pass its doors every day just as crowds of immigrants once passed down the street. Most of the buildings added over the years were torn down in 1963 to make way for the university.

Through the Hull-House Association and the Women's International League for Peace and Freedom, Jane Addams was a good neighbor to those who lived on her block and to those who lived halfway across the world. The Women's League continues to work for human rights and peace. The Hull-House Association also continues its work with programs, organizations, and community centers all over the Chicago area. Today it survives as a source of hope and help to people in the city, just as Jane would have wished.

Notes

page 10

Jennie's father was surprised and amused by her reaction to the "horrid little houses." He told the story often while she was growing up. Like many stories passed down through the years, it probably changed in the telling. When Jane Addams wrote her autobiography, she may have been remembering a family legend more than the actual event.

page 15

For the sake of clarity, Jane Addams is referred to as Jane throughout this book. But she was formal as well as friendly. Even among her college friends, she usually preferred to be called Miss Addams instead of Jane. Some Hull-House residents, such as Florence Kelley and Julia Lathrop, called her J.A.

page 22

Jane Addams described the food auction and her reaction to it more powerfully in her autobiography than she did in letters she wrote to her family from Europe. Thinking back to the auction years later, it may have seemed even worse to her than it did at the time. Perhaps she did not write all her feelings in the letters. Or perhaps she simply wanted to make her book as interesting as possible for her readers.

page 25

Some historians do not think the bullfight was as important in motivating Jane as she seems to remember. Whether or not they are right, something happened in Europe to set her on the course that eventually led to Hull-House. Her visit to Toynbee Hall in London probably had a lot to do with shaping her ideas.

page 38

Hull-House is spelled with a hyphen in this book because that is the way Jane Addams spelled it. In many sources, however, it is spelled without the hyphen.

page 53

Some of Hull-House's early projects included a coffeehouse, public baths, and a drugstore that sold medicine at bargain rates. Through the years, Hull-House residents investigated the causes of diseases, such as tuberculosis and typhoid fever. They studied the quality of Chicago's milk supply and the problem of children who did not go to school. They helped establish Chicago's first public swimming pool, first Boy Scout troop, and one of the country's first amateur theaters. After the Factory Act was repealed, residents worked for the passage of the Illinois Child Labor Act, which became law in 1903.

page 64

When Theodore Roosevelt did not receive the Republican party nomination for president in 1912, he and his followers decided to form a new party, the Progressives. But by the next election year, the Progressive party had disappeared from the political scene.

page 85

Jane Addams shared the Nobel Peace Prize with an industrialist named Nicholas Murray Butler.

BIBLIOGRAPHY

Books:

Addams, Jane. *Peace and Bread in Time of War.* New York: Garland Publishing, 1972.

Addams, Jane. *The Second Twenty Years at Hull-House, September 1909 to September 1929, with a Record of a Growing World Consciousness.* New York: The MacMillan Company, 1930.

Addams, Jane. *Twenty Years at Hull House with Autobiographical Notes.* Urbana: University of Illinois Press, 1990.

Addams, Jane; Emily G. Balch, and Alice Hamilton. *Women at The Hague: The International Congress of Women and Its Results.* New York: Garland Publishing, 1972.

Bryan, Mary Lynn McCree, and Allen F. Davis, editors. *100 Years at Hull-House.* Bloomington: Indiana University Press, 1990.

Davis, Allen F. *American Heroine: The Life and Legend of Jane Addams.* New York: Oxford University Press, 1973.

Farrell, John C. *Beloved Lady: A History of Jane Addams' Ideas on Reform and Peace.* Baltimore, Maryland: Johns Hopkins Press, 1967.

Hamilton, Alice. *Exploring the Dangerous Trades: The Autobiography of Alice Hamilton.* Boston: Little, Brown, and Company, 1943.

Hirsch, Susan E., and Robert I. Goler. *A City Comes of Age: Chicago in the 1890s.* Chicago: Chicago Historical Society, 1990.

Holli, Melvin G., et al. *Opening New Worlds: Jane Addams' Hull House.* Chicago: University of Illinois Press, 1989.

Johnson, Emily Cooper, editor. *Jane Addams: A Centennial Reader.* New York: MacMillan Company, 1960.

*Kittredge, Mary. *Jane Addams: Social Worker.* New York: Chelsea House Publishers, 1988.

Lasch, Christopher. *The Social Thought of Jane Addams.* Indianapolis: The Bobbs-Merrill Company, 1965.

Levine, Daniel. *Jane Addams and the Liberal Tradition.* Madison: State Historical Society of Wisconsin, 1971.

Linn, James Weber. *Jane Addams: A Biography.* New York: Greenwood Press, 1968.

*Meigs, Cornelia. *Jane Addams: Pioneer for Social Justice.* Boston: Little, Brown, and Company, 1970.

Polacheck, Hilda Satt. Edited by Dena J. Polacheck Epstein. *I Came a Stranger: The Story of a Hull-House Girl.* Urbana: University of Illinois Press, 1989.

Manuscripts:

Addams, Jane. Scrapbooks. Photocopies of three scrapbooks of clippings and programs compiled by Addams during the early years of Hull-House. The Jane Addams Memorial Collection, University of Illinois, Chicago.

Fry, Paul E. "Generous Spirit: The Life of Mary Fry." Privately published manuscript. Courtesy of the Cedarville Historical Society.

*A star denotes a book for younger readers.

All quotations in this biography were taken from the above sources.

Index

Hull-House kids on Halloween in the 1940s

Illustrations are reproduced through the courtesy of: Rockford College Archives, pp. 2, 13, 16, 17; Swarthmore College Peace Collection, p. 6; Jane Addams Memorial Collection, Special Collections, The University Library, The University of Illinois at Chicago, pp. 9, 11, 14, 21, 25, 30, 32, 34, 36, 41, 43 (both, Wallace Kirkland Papers), 44, 49, 57 (Wallace Kirkland Papers), 59 (Wallace Kirkland Papers), 60, 81, 83 (both, Wallace Kirkland Papers), 84 (Wallace Kirkland Papers), 86, 89, 95, front cover (street scene), back cover; Archives and Special Collections on Women in Medicine, Medical College of Pennsylvania, p. 19; The Library of Congress, pp. 46, 62, 64 (Photo by American Press Association), 69, front cover (portrait); Chicago Historical Society, p. 51; *The Boston Journal,* p. 66; Sophia Smith Collection, Smith College, p. 72.

Excerpts from *I Came a Stranger: The Story of a Hull-House Girl* by Hilda Satt Polacheck, edited by Dena J. Polacheck Epstein (Urbana: University of Illinois Press, 1989), appear on pages 39, 44, 54, 84-85, and 86 (caption).